Pythons

by Mary Ann McDonald

Illustrated with photographs
by Joe McDonald

Capstone Press

MINNEAPOLIS

Printed in the United States of America.

Capstone Press • 2440 Fernbrook Lane • Minneapolis, MN 55447

Editorial Director   John Coughlan
Managing Editor   Tom Streissguth
Production Editor   Jim Stapleton
Book Designer   Timothy Halldin

Library of Congress Cataloging-in-Publication Data
McDonald, Mary Ann.
   Pythons / by Mary Ann and Joe McDonald; illustrated with photographs by the authors.
          p. cm.
   Includes bibliographical references (p. 46) and index.
   Summary: Describes the physical characteristics, habitat, and different varieties of pythons.
   ISBN 1-56065-296-9
   1. Pythons--Juvenile literature. [1. Pythons. 2. Snakes.] I. McDonald, Joe. II. Title
   QL666.O63M34 1996
   597.96--dc20   95-438
                                                     CIP
                                                     AC
00 99 98 97   8 7 6 5 4 3 2

Table of Contents

Fast Facts about Pythons

Description: Pythons are some of the largest snakes in the world. They range in length from the huge reticulated python down to Liasis perthensis, an Australian species that is only 20 inches (50 centimeters) long. The longest snake ever recorded was a reticulated python measuring almost 33 feet (10 meters) long.

Scientific name: Pythons belong to the family Boidae, to which boa **constrictors** and anacondas also belong.

Range: Pythons are found throughout Africa, southern Asia, Indonesia, and Australia.

Food: Pythons eat frogs, small mammals, birds, and larger animals like monkeys and small antelopes.

Habitat: Pythons live in many habitats, including deserts, tropical rain forests, and open brushlands.

Distinctive habits: Pythons are constrictors. They kill by squeezing the air out of their prey's lungs and preventing the prey from breathing.

Reproduction: Pythons lay eggs, sometimes up to 100 at a time. The female incubates the eggs by coiling her body around them.

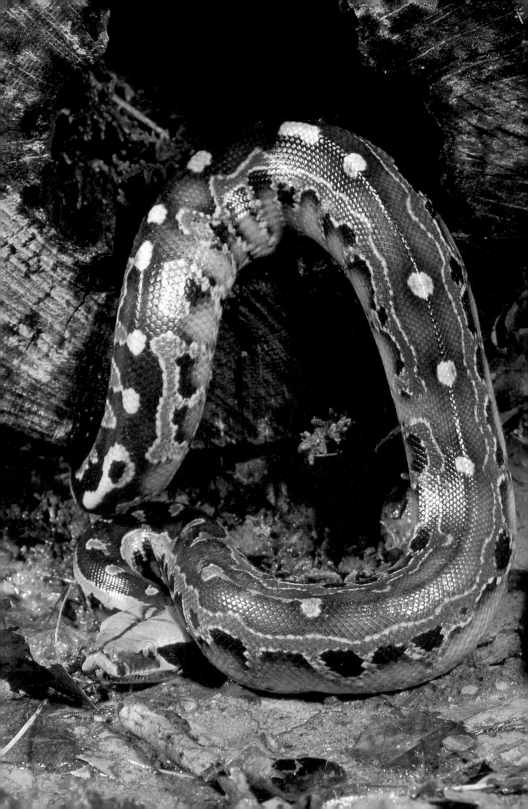

Chapter 1
The Python

Pythons live in warm and tropical parts of Africa, southern Asia, and Australia. Their habitats include deserts, open brushlands, and tropical rain forests. Some pythons are **arboreal**, meaning they live in trees. Most large python species live on the ground. Others are **fossorial**—they live underground.

Some python species reach lengths of between 21 feet (6.5 meters) and 33 feet (10 meters). The larger species of pythons can be

The blood python lives in the tropical forests of Indonesia.

The arboreal green tree python prefers life in the trees.

dangerous. In Asia, there are records of pythons eating small children.

Because of their large size, pythons can't move very fast or very far. But they do have many different color patterns that help them to hide, if necessary. This **camouflage** allows them to blend in with their surroundings.

8

How Pythons Adapt

The green tree python lives in the rain forests of Papua New Guinea and northern Australia. This bright green arboreal snake has adapted to life in the trees with a **prehensile tail**. The tail wraps around a branch several times to anchor the snake on its perch.

In many ways, the emerald tree boa of South America is similar to the green tree python. Although they are not closely related, both live in jungle trees. They also have the same colors and eating habits. Two different species sometimes develop in the same way, even if they live in different parts of the world. This is called **parallel evolution**.

Chapter 2

Size, Color, and Shape

Pythons are among the largest and strongest snakes in the world. The African and Indian pythons are both very large snakes. While pythons are the longest snakes, anacondas are the heaviest. Some anacondas weigh more than 300 pounds (136 kilograms).

Pythons range in color from brown and black to red, orange, or green. The green tree python is very unusual. Its young are bright yellow or brick red. When they are two years old, their color changes to bright green.

The ball python, which reaches a length of about five feet, makes a popular pet among snake lovers.

This Burmese python is an albino, meaning it has no color pigment in its scales.

Many **albinos** can be found among captive pythons. An albino python doesn't have the normal color cells. Instead, albinos have red eyes and a light yellow skin. In the wild, white pythons would be unable to hide from prey or enemies. They would die of starvation or be quickly killed.

Pythons have many different camouflage patterns. This type of pattern, called **disruptive coloration**, makes the snake hard to see along a trail or on the forest floor. You could easily walk past a 20-foot (6-meter) python and not even see it lying in the leaves. Because pythons hide so well, some scientists believe that some unknown species of python may still exist.

The small royal python has a different way of defending itself. It rolls up in a tight ball with its head in the center of its coils. This habit has earned it the nickname of the "ball python."

Scales and Skin

Thousands of small scales cover most of the python's body, including its head and even its

Color patterns change from species to species and even from snake to snake.

eyes. There are larger scales on its belly. These scales have a color pattern that is different from those on its back and sides.

Snakes grow their entire lives. As they grow, they shed the outer layer of their skin. Young pythons eat more, grow faster, and shed more often than adults. Right after the snake sheds, its skin is shiny and beautiful.

The skin of a snake is made up of thousands of tiny scales.

Color patterns sometimes make it hard to tell where the snake's head is.

The Python's Body

A python's body is slightly flat on the bottom. With a flat belly, the snake can use more of its **scutes**, or large belly scales, to move itself.

The python's skeleton is made up of a skull, a long backbone, and hundreds of ribs. Large pythons can have as many as 500 vertebrae, or back bones. The more vertebrae a python has, the stronger and more flexible it is.

A python has a heart, stomach, liver, kidney, and lungs, just as we do. But the snake's organs are long and slender. The tail makes up a small part of the snake's length.

Pythons and boas evolved from lizards a long time ago. Over time, the lizards lost their front and back legs. But pythons and boas still have two small back legs, called spurs, near their tails. These spurs look like claws.

Loners

Pythons live alone most of their lives. Unlike many other snakes, they don't hibernate in the winter. They gather only during courtship and mating. Female pythons will guard their eggs and newly hatched young. But just a few days after the young hatch, the female leaves them. Then the babies must survive on their own.

Scales cover even the eyes of the green tree python.

Chapter 3

Movement

The large, heavy python doesn't move very fast. Most of the time, it just lies patiently and waits for its prey. When it moves, it usually goes in a straight line.

Most large snakes, including pythons, use **caterpillar motion**. In caterpillar motion, the python's rib muscles raise and lower its scutes into the ground. A rippling action of the muscles puts many of the scutes into the soil at once. The python uses the rippling action to pull its body forward.

Smaller pythons and the young of large pythons sometimes use **serpentine motion**.

The emerald tree boa moves easily along a branch.

The snake pushes off rough surfaces with both
its belly and sides. Whatever path the head
takes, the body and tail follow right behind.
Small pythons use this type of locomotion to
move fast.

Moving in the Trees
   Green tree pythons are strong tree climbers.
Using their prehensile tails, they can hang onto

one branch while reaching across to another. In this way, a python can stretch out at least half of its body length.

Using its chin to brace on the new branch, the python begins to cross the opening. Its strong muscles keep it straight as it stretches toward the new tree. When the body is halfway across, the snake lets go with its tail. The python's tail gently glides straight across the opening to the new branch. The python never lets its tail dangle from the tree. A waving tail could attract a predator or throw the snake off balance.

Living Underground

Several species of pythons live in the ground. One very small Australian species lives in termite mounds. Here it hunts for the gecko, a type of lizard that eats termites.

Pythons that burrow in the ground usually have a blunt or flattened head and tail. This helps the snake shovel into and through soil or sand.

Chapter 4

The Senses

Without arms or legs, pythons have developed unusual sense organs that help them survive. Although some of these organs are similar to ours, others are quite different.

Some pythons have two rows of special heat-sensitive holes, or pits, on each side of their heads. These pits lie in the middle of the python's upper lip scales. They follow the heat produced by warm-blooded animals and help the python find food. Many pythons hunt at night using only their pits to track prey.

Sight and Smell

Pythons have very poor eyesight. Like most snakes, they can't focus more than two feet (61 centimeters) away. Because they can't see very clearly, they react to movement when they hunt for food.

The eyes of pythons have vertical pupils. At night, these pupils open so wide that they look almost round. This allows more light into the eyes and helps the snake see better in the dark.

Pythons smell in two ways. They have nostrils that smell just as human nostrils do.

Two heat-sensing pits in the front of a python's head help it to track prey.

The forked tongue helps the snake smell for scents in the dust.

They also use their long, forked tongues to smell, or taste, different scents. They flick their tongues very slowly in the air or along the ground. The tongue picks up small pieces of dust. The python draws its tongue back in its mouth and rubs it against special glands, called **Jacobson's organs**, on the roof of the mouth.

The Jacobson's organs send these scent messages to the python's brain, which sorts out all of the different smells. The python can use its sense of smell to find prey or other pythons.

Two Burmese pythons—one albino, the other normally colored—cross paths.

By following a scent trail, pythons can even follow prey down into their burrows.

Snakes can't hear noises as humans do because they don't have external ears. They feel, or "hear," vibrations by laying their head on the ground. Through their jawbones, the vibrations are sent to their inner ears. Pythons feel animals or people coming long before they see them.

The python uses all of these senses to hunt. Often, they first feel the vibrations of approaching prey. Their pits also pick up heat from animals at a distance. As the prey gets closer, the python may smell it with its tongue or nostrils. Finally, the python will see the prey when it gets very close.

The python also uses its senses to protect itself. When a python senses a large mammal coming, it has time to hide or to become still. Its camouflage protects the python from discovery.

Chapter 5

Hunting

Many pythons are too large to hunt actively. Instead, they lie by a path or waterhole. The python may wait for hours or even days for its prey.

The larger the python, the larger the animal it can eat. An adult python might even attack leopards or antelopes. An African rock python weighing around 140 pounds (63.5 kilograms) once ate an animal that weighed more than 130 pounds (59 kilograms).

After eating a large animal, the python becomes very thick and has difficulty moving. Instead, the snake finds a safe place and curls

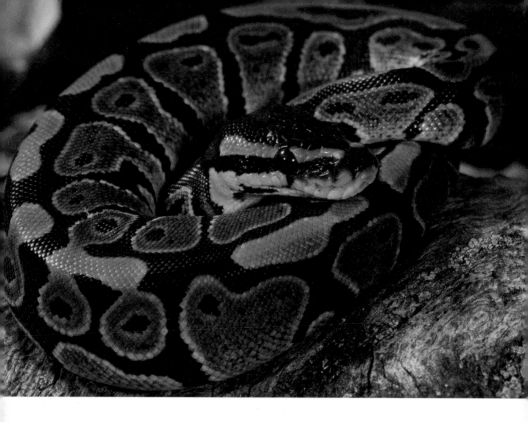

up to let its food digest. If a python eats a very large animal, it may not have to eat again for months or even a year.

Hunting and Eating

A python has six rows of sharp teeth that curve backward in its mouth. The teeth help the snake hold and swallow its prey. The python quickly strikes its victim and then holds the prey in its mouth. Even slippery prey can't break loose from the snake's jaws.

Once the python has a good grip, it throws one or more coils around the animal. The python then squeezes the animal to death. This process is called **constriction**. Every time the animal exhales air, the python squeezes tighter. Every breath becomes harder. The animal eventually dies from lack of oxygen.

Anacondas, the world's heaviest snakes, easily swim through swampy waters.

The python can squeeze so hard that the eyes of its prey bulge out. Sometimes small bones, like a thin leg bone, will break. But this is never the main cause of death.

After its prey dies, the python slowly uncoils. Using its tongue, the snake searches for the head of the animal. It is important for the python to eat its prey head first. By eating this way, the arms and legs of the prey fold back and don't get stuck in the snake's throat.

Since a python has no hands to help stuff the meal into its mouth, its jaws must do all the work. By moving the right and left sides of each jaw in turn, the python works the food into its mouth and down into its stomach.

Arboreal pythons eat birds, tree frogs, eggs, and sometimes monkeys. Fossorial pythons eat rodents, lizards, and other snakes. Large, ground-dwelling pythons eat rodents, small mammals, other snakes, small antelopes, wild pigs, and monkeys.

A carpet python lazes on a comfortable log.

Chapter 6

Reproduction

Pythons are solitary, living alone all of their life. After hatching, young pythons may stay together near the nest for a few days. But soon they wander off on their own. Adult pythons only come together to mate.

When a female is ready to mate, she will leave a scent trail. The male python follows this trail with his tongue and Jacobson's organs. When the male finds the female, they go through a small courting ceremony.

The Mating Dance

During the courtship, the male rubs his chin along the female's body. He will also use his spurs to tickle the female around her tail. When the female is ready, she raises her tail. The two pythons intertwine and mate.

Two Burmese pythons meet and mate.

Like birds, pythons are **oviparous**, meaning they lay eggs. The number of eggs varies. The small Angolan and royal pythons lay only five to eight eggs. The larger reticulated and

A blood python from Indonesia tests the air for telltale scents.

African rock pythons sometimes lay up to 100 eggs at one time.

Most snakes abandon the eggs once they are laid. But pythons incubate their eggs. After laying her eggs, the female coils her body around them. This protects the eggs from enemies and keeps them warm. Incubation lasts as long as 100 days. During this time, the female only leaves the eggs to drink.

In and Out of the Egg

The oblong python egg is soft and leathery. As the young snake grows inside the egg, it may double in size. Oxygen and water, which can enter the egg through the shell, are very important to the growing snake.

The female doesn't help her babies hatch. Each baby has a hard white tooth on the end of its nose. The young snake will use this egg tooth to make several slits in the shell. It crawls out of one of these slits. After several weeks, the young snake's egg tooth falls off.

Growing Up

Life is dangerous for young pythons. They have many enemies, including hawks, eagles, other snakes, turtles, and some mammals. They spend most of their time hiding from their enemies.

Pythons can live a very long time. In captivity, they can live as long as 75 years. Nobody knows how long pythons live in the wild.

Chapter 7

Pythons and Humans

Snake worship has been part of human history since early times. Snakes were important to the aborigines of Australia, to the Egyptians, and to the ancient tribes of Central and South America. They were worshipped as gods and used in religious ceremonies.

Pythons can be tame in captivity. Because of this, many people keep pythons as pets. They may buy a young python that measures 18 inches (46 centimeters). But they may not realize that some pythons can grow as long as 21 feet (6.5 meters) and can live more than 50

Snake handlers must always be careful around large pythons and other constrictors.

years. Ball pythons, which measure only up to five feet (1.5 meters), are a favorite among snake owners.

Python owners must be very careful. A large snake may get scared and suddenly wrap itself around its owner, who could be accidentally killed by his or her pet.

Owners should know proper care and feeding of the ball python or of any other pet snake they keep.

Taking Care of a Pet Python

Keeping a pet snake is a lot of work. As the snake grows, it will need a large cage and larger meals. It's not easy to find a whole chicken, with feathers, to feed a 13-foot (four-meter) pet.

Pythons at Risk

Illegal trade in snake meat and snakeskins is threatening many snake species. Pythons in southeast Asia are in danger. Because large pythons can't crawl very fast, it is easy for villagers to catch them.

Pythons eat rodents, especially rats, which can carry disease. For this reason, people in many countries like to have pythons living around their barns and grain-stores.

Conservationists hope that pythons will continue to survive in the wild. We can help by closing down the illegal snake business. People who want to own a python should buy one that was born in captivity. And anyone who buys a snake should know how to care for it.

Glossary

albino–an animal lacking the color cells needed for its natural color. An albino's eyes are red, its hair white, and its skin a pale white or light yellow.

arboreal–animals that live or hunt in trees

camouflage–patterns and colors that help an animal hide

caterpillar motion–a motion used by snakes, especially larger ones, to move in a straight line

constriction–suffocating an animal by squeezing it

constrictors–snakes that kill their prey by squeezing and suffocating them

disruptive coloration–patterns of color that break up an animal's outline, making it harder to see

fossorial–animals that live or hunt underground

Jacobson's organs–special glands in a snake's mouth that help the snake to taste, or smell, different scents

oviparous–egg-laying

parallel evolution–unrelated species that live in similar habitats and have evolved to look and act alike

prehensile tail–a tail that can wrap tightly around an object, like a tree branch

scutes–the large belly scales of a snake

serpentine motion–a motion used by snakes to move along rough surfaces

spurs–small, claw-like legs of a python or boa

vertebrae–back bones

To Learn More

Arnold, Caroline. *Snake.* New York: Morrow Jr. Books, 1991.

Freedman, Russel. *Killer Snakes.* New York: Holiday House, 1982.

Gross, Ruth Below. *Snakes.* New York: Four Winds Press, 1990.

Simon, Seymour. *Snakes.* New York: Harper Collins, 1992.

Smith, Roland. *Snakes in the Zoo.* Brookfield, CT: Millbrook Press, 1992.

Magazines:

Reptiles and Amphibians
Reptiles

Some Useful Addresses

Sonora Desert Museum
2021 N. Kinney Rd.
Tucson, Arizona   85743

Clyde Peelings Reptiland
Route 15
Allenwood, PA   17810

National Zoological Park
3001 Connecticut Avenue NW
Washington, DC   20008

Toronto Zoo
361A Old Finch Avenue
Scarborough, Ontario M1B 5K7

Dallas Zoo
621 E. Clarendon
Dallas, TX   75203

Index

African rock python, 29, 37
albinos, 12
anacondas, 5, 11

ball pythons, 41-42
boa constrictors, 5, 16

camouflage, 8, 12, 27
caterpillar motion, 19
colors, 8-9, 11
constriction, 31

eggs, 12, 14, 24
emerald tree boa, 9
eyes, 12, 14, 24

food, 5

green tree python, 9, 11,
  20-21

habitat, 5, 7
hunting, 23-24, 27, 29-32

Jacobson's organs, 25, 35
jawbones, 26

mating, 17, 35-36

pits, 23, 27

reproduction, 5, 35-39
reticulated python, 4-5, 37
royal python, 13, 37

scales, 13-15
scutes, 15, 19
serpentine motion, 19-20
shedding, 14
skin, 12, 14
smell, 24-26
spurs, 16, 36

teeth, 31, 39
tongues, 25, 27, 32, 35

48

The streamlined body of the mako makes it one of the fastest sharks in the water.

The keel of a boat sticks down into the water from the boat's bottom. The keel of a mako sticks out to the sides, giving it more power. Many strong muscles in the mako's tail are attached to the keel. So it plays an important part in helping the shark to swim fast and powerfully.

14

Important Gills

Most fish get oxygen through gills instead of through lungs. Mako sharks have five large **gill slits** on the side of the body. Water enters the slits and passes over the thin gills. The gills take oxygen from the water.

A mako's gill slits are extra long, so that the shark can get the extra oxygen its body needs for its bursts of speed.

Their warm bodies also help makos move at top speed. Most fish lose heat from their blood through their gills. Makos and their relatives do not. The heat stays in the body, keeping the muscles ready for action.

Makos are so famous for speed that people who see any fast shark may call it a mako.

Meet the Real Mako

The mako shark belongs to a small group of sharks called mackerel sharks. The famed man-eating great white shark is also a mackerel shark.

Mackerel sharks were probably named for mackerel fish, because both have a keel at the base of the tail. But a mackerel is a bony fish. Its skeleton is made of bones, like a human's.

Sharks, however, have no bones. Instead, they are made up of **cartilage**. Cartilage is softer than bone, but it is still stiff. Humans have cartilage in their noses, ears, and kneecaps.

The mako is also called the sharp-nosed mackerel shark or the shortfin mako. The fin on its side (its **pectoral** fin) is shorter than the one on its closest relative, the longfin mako.

Where They Live

Mako sharks live in all the major oceans of the world. They like warm or almost warm water. They often stay in the region where cold and warm ocean water meet. There are a lot of fish there for them to catch.

For a long time, scientists thought that the mako of the Atlantic Ocean and the mako of the Pacific were different **species**, or kinds, of

Gill slits on the sides of the mako allow the fish to take in oxygen.

shark. Now they know that shortfin makos are the same all over the world.

Makos swim in deep waters. They don't often come close to shore. That is why swimmers don't often see them.

That's a good thing, because makos can be very dangerous!

Chapter 2

The Mako Eating Machine

Powerful makos need a lot of food for energy. These sharks spend most of their lives hunting for food.

Different sharks eat different foods. What they like depends partly on where they live. Makos live out in the open sea. Their bodies and their teeth are made for catching fast fish and other animals.

Makos stay very busy hunting food. They eat many times their own weight every year. Sometimes a mako will swim through a school

The lower teeth of a mako shark look like curved daggers.

of fish with its mouth open, gulping down whole fish as fast as it can.

Growing Up

The things makos eat change as they grow. Smaller makos (up to about 300 pounds, or 136 kilograms) have long, pointed teeth. They use them to catch fish and squid. Mackerel make a nice meal for smaller makos.

As sharks get bigger, their teeth get bigger, too. They become more like knives. A big mako can eat big fish such as swordfish and marlin. They may catch dolphins or seals.

A mako does not chew its food. It usually swallows its prey whole. One time a whole 120-pound (54-kilogram) swordfish was found inside the stomach of a 700-pound (318-kilogram) mako.

Mako Teeth

Most sharks have teeth that angle backward into their mouths when their mouths are closed. But a mako's bottom teeth always stand upright. Its lower teeth look like curved daggers that stick up from its lower jaw. This makes a mako frightening when seen up close.

Many sharks have teeth that are jagged, or **serrated**, like a saw blade, on the sides. A mako's teeth are more like smooth knives. They are not serrated. The knife-like teeth can easily grasp large prey.

Makos have eight rows of teeth in their jaws. The front row is used for eating. When a

Blue on top and silvery on the bottom, the mako disguises itself by blending into the water's changing colors.

shark loses a front tooth, another one moves up from behind to replace it. Sometimes this new tooth, fully grown, moves into place in only 24 hours!

Sharks' teeth are often found on beaches. In New Zealand, the native people often wore mako teeth to decorate their ears.

Fast-Moving Meals

Makos are the fastest sharks. So it's not surprising that they eat fast-moving fish. Makos go after other sharks, tunas, herring, squid, mackerel, bluefish, and swordfish.

Swordfish are big, even as big as a big shark. But that doesn't stop makos from chasing them for a good meal. Makos have

Makos hunt and attack using all six of their senses.

been known to go after swordfish one-third their own size. Makos have been caught with the whole sword from a swordfish hanging off their flesh.

Hearing and Touching

Sharks have ears for hearing sound. But you can't see an outer ear on a shark's head. The hearing organ is hidden away behind the thick skin of the head. It is very sensitive. It can hear sounds much lower in pitch than people can hear.

Sharks also have a special sense that is like both hearing and touch. Running along the side of the shark's body and into its head and inner ear is a strip of sensing cells. This special sensory strip is called the **lateral line**.

The lateral line senses motion in the water. Sharks use the lateral line to become aware of moving fish and other distant motion. They can sense movements that are too small for humans to see.

Seeing the Light

Eyesight is not very important to many sharks. But sharks do see some colors. They like bright colors, like the bright orange used on life vests. Sharks are so attracted to this color that scientists call it "yum-yum yellow."

Mako sharks have mirror-like cells in the back of their eyes. Cats also have this layer of cells. The cells reflect light back, making them glow in only a little light. The special cells help sharks see in the dim light of the ocean.

The Sixth Sense

Sharks have another sense that no other animal has. Tiny pores, or holes, on their heads are filled with a watery fluid. These pores are called **ampullae of Lorenzini**. (An ampoule is a small bottle). The man who discovered them was named Lorenzini.

All living creatures give off tiny electrical signals. The moving muscles of animals give off an especially good signal. Ampullae of Lorenzini can sense these electrical signals from moving fish.

A mako can see, smell, hear, detect motion, and sense electrical signals. This makes them very dangerous hunters.

Wounded prey send out even stronger electrical signals. So sharks zoom in on them. Sometimes sharks have kept attacking the same victim, even if another fish gets closer. Scientists believe this is because of the strong electrical signal the wounded victim is sending out.

Putting the Senses to Work

Sharks use all their senses in hunting.

First, they smell their prey. Often they smell the blood of a wounded, bleeding animal.

In wartime, when ships have exploded, sharks were drawn to the wounded men in the water. Sharks can also "hear" the low sounds of splashing fish (or swimmers).

When a hunting mako gets closer to possible food, vision kicks in. Sharks can tell light from dark and some colors.

But they are more likely to actually locate their prey when the ampullae of Lorenzini start to buzz. Then the shark can pick up the prey's electrical signals. A shark might actually bump into its prey by using this sense.

The shark might then take a bite–but it is still testing. The shark might decide it doesn't want what its senses led it to. It will spit out its catch and swim away.

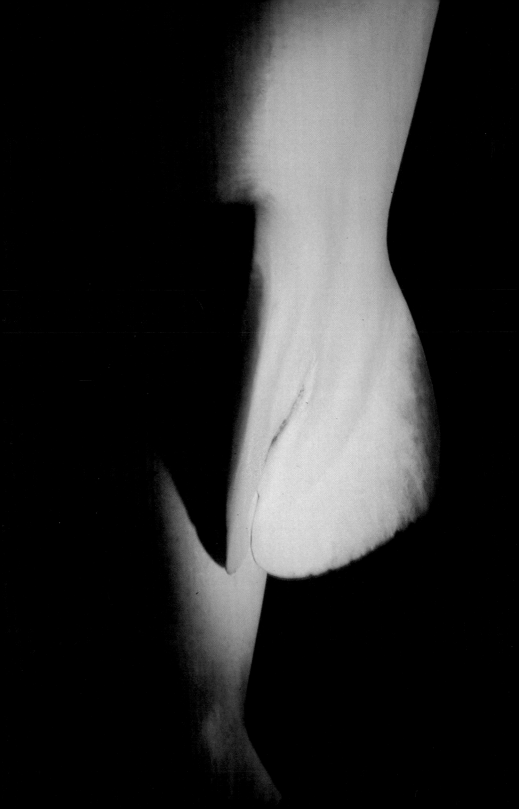

Chapter 3
The Life of a Mako

Young mako sharks grow faster than most other sharks. The pups often grow about a foot each year until they are full grown.

Makos swim the oceans all alone, except when they mate. A male will be ready to mate when it is about 6.5 feet (2 meters) long. A female will be bigger, about 8.5 feet (2.6 meters).

Mating Habits

Most female fish lay eggs, which are fertilized when the male releases sperm over them. But mako eggs are fertilized inside the female.

The female mako lays eggs through the cloaca, between her pelvic fins.

When a male mako happens to find a willing female, he approaches and bumps her. He bites her hard, leaving deep scars.

Male sharks use special organs called **claspers** to mate with females. Claspers look rather like small fins on their abdomens. They are used to hold onto the female.

The male slides one clasper into an opening on the female. Then a channel inside the clasper sends sperm into the female's body, where it fertilizes the eggs.

From Eggs to Young

Mako eggs hatch inside the mother. The hatched young, called pups, continue to grow inside, nice and warm. They eat other eggs that the mother's body keeps producing. In fact, they eat so much that they are born with fat stomachs filled with food. This keeps them going for several days.

The claspers of the male mako are used in mating.

A shark gives birth to its pups along the ocean floor.

When mako pups are about 26 inches (65 centimeters) long, the pups are born. They are born ready to start swimming.

The mako shark usually gives birth to 4 or 5 pups. Most sharks have 6 to 12 pups. But some, like the tiger and hammerhead, have as many as 40.

Out into the World

The pups set off on their own adventures in the oceans of the world. They begin to hunt for food right away. Makos hunt at both dusk and dawn, when their prey might be waking up or tired from the day. The sharks themselves probably never sleep.

Scientists don't know how long makos live. Their average age could range from 5 to 12 years old. Or they might live to be as old as 50 years. They probably die when they've used up all their eight rows of teeth and can no longer eat.

Chapter 4

Attack! Fighting for Their Lives

Makos are legends. They are the most exciting fish a fisherman can go after for sport. Books have been written about the fierce battles these game fish have fought to avoid being caught.

When hooked, makos fight long and hard for their lives. And they are **aggressive**. They are the only big-game fish that can bring real danger to the person fishing.

Scientists haul in a mako shark for further examination.

Makos are a challenge to catch, but they also taste good. Their flesh is the best-tasting of all shark meat. Mako is often served in fine restaurants.

In North America, there is good fishing for makos in the Atlantic Ocean off New York. Fishermen also find them in the Gulf of Mexico off Texas.

But the best mako fishing is near Australia and New Zealand. In fact, the native people of New Zealand, called Maori, gave the shark its name of mako.

Leaping for Freedom

A mako's powerful tail helps it to swim very fast, but it also helps it do something else. The mako can use its tail to make a fantastic

This mako was caught during a fishing tournament.

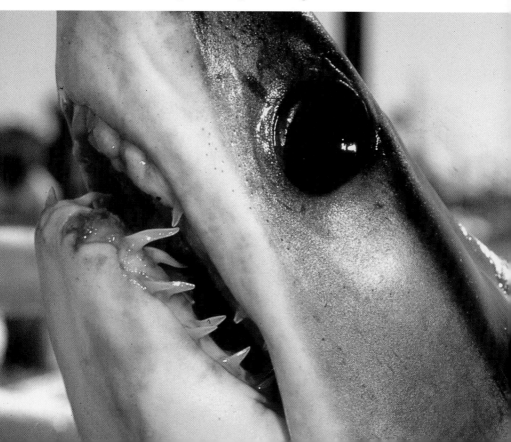

leap out of the water while trying to get rid of the hook.

A mako has been known to surge out of the sea to a height of 20 feet (6 meters). Some fisherman have claimed that a mako had to leap 30 feet (9 meters) high in order to get over his boat. To do that, the shark must get a running start of at least 22 miles (35 kilometers) per hour.

Once, a man speared a mako in shallow water off the coast of Puerto Rico. The mako swam to deeper water, shook out the spear, and came back to the shore. It jumped right onto the shore at the man's feet. Then it jumped back into the ocean and was gone before anyone could catch it.

Attack

When leaping does not free the shark, its anger may make it attack the fishing boat as if it were a living enemy. Deep-sea fishing boats are usually too strong to be harmed by the

A diver wears a steel suit before mingling with a group of hungry sharks.

shark. But makos often leave some of their teeth in the boats.

Makos even have jumped right onto a boat deck and attacked the fisherman! They thrash around the deck, putting the fisherman in danger, until they surge back into the water. If the shark accidentally knocks the fisherman in the water, the fisherman can be in serious danger of being attacked.

The Shark Attack File

In 1958, a group of scientists formed the Shark Research Panel. They wanted to learn as much as they could about sharks. They also created the Shark Attack File. It contained reports and photographs of all known shark attacks. Most reports were not able to name the shark that attacked.

The Shark Attack File is no longer kept, but it revealed a lot about sharks.

Because sharks are made of cartilage, and not bone, nothing remains of them but their teeth.

Of the more than 370 types of sharks, only about 30 are dangerous to humans. Only three types of sharks account for most attacks. These are the great white, the tiger, and the bull shark.

About 20 makos attacked people while the Shark Attack File was kept. Usually, the people got in the way when a mako attacked a boat. Makos rarely swim in water shallow enough for swimmers, but they sometimes do so in Australia. There the swimmers must beware!

People are lucky that makos usually live so far out at sea. They are large, fast, and ferocious. If it liked shallow water, the mako shark might be even more dangerous than the great white!

Glossary

aggressive–full of energy; determined; willing to fight

ampullae of Lorenzini–fluid-filled sacs in sharks that can sense vibrations and help sharks "hear"

cartilage–a stiff but bendable body tissue. Sharks have a skeleton made of cartilage instead of bone.

claspers–a pair of organs located on the abdomen on a male shark, used for mating. They look like extra fins.

dorsal–located on the back of the shark, such as fins

gill slits–the long, straight openings on the side of a shark, into which water flows. A mako has five large gill slits.

keel–a flat part of the body that sticks out from another part, like the keel of a boat. A mako's keel strengthens its tail.

lateral line–a row of special sensory cells that is present along the side of a shark. It senses motion in the water

pectoral–located on the sides of the shark, such as fins

serrated–saw-toothed

species–a certain kind of animal or plant. Usually, creatures of one species only mate with each other.

streamlined–smooth-shaped for low resistance and fast movement through air or water

To Learn More

Blassingame, Wyatt. *Wonders of Sharks.* New York: Dodd, Mead, and Co., 1984.

Cerullo, Mary M. *Sharks: Challengers of the Deep.* New York: Cobblehill Books, 1993.

Freedman, Russel. *Sharks.* New York: Holiday House, 1985.

Langley, Andrew. *The World of Sharks.* New York: Bookwright Press, 1987.

Springer Victor G. and Joy P. Gould. *Sharks In Question: The Smithsonian Answer Book.* 1989.

Steel, Rodney. *Sharks of the World.* New York: Facts on File, 1989.

Sharks, Silent Hunters of the Deep. Readers Digest, 1987.

About the Author

Anne Welsbacher is publications director at the Science Museum of Minnesota. She writes science articles for various publications and is a playwright.

Index

muscles, 15

New York, 36
New Zealand, 22, 37

oxygen, 14-15

Pacific Ocean, 16
porbeagles, 4

Puerto Rico, 38

range, 5, 16-17
scientific names, 4, 11
seals, 21
senses, 24-27, 43-44
Shark Attack File, 41-42
Shark Research Panel,
    41
skeletons, 15, 43

skin, 11, 24
snouts, 7-8
speed, 7-9, 15, 23, 38
squid, 20, 23
swordfish, 21, 23-24

tails, 8, 11, 14-15, 37, 43
teeth, 4, 7, 9, 19-22, 33,
    41
Texas, 36
tiger sharks, 42
tunas, 23

Virginia, 9

weight, 5, 9, 20-21
West Indies, 9